FRANZ JOSEF
HAYDN

THREE TRIOS
for PIANO, VIOLIN (OR FLUTE) *and* VIOLONCELLO

G MAJOR  G-

HOB. XV:25

F-SHARP MAJOR FIS-DUR

HOB. XV:26

F MAJOR F-DUR

HOB. XV:6

Music Minus One

3076

Music Minus One

3076

CONTENTS

ISBN 978-1-59615-070-6

TRIO
for PIANO, VIOLIN (OR FLUTE) and VIOLONCELLO
G MAJOR 𝄵 G-DUR
HOB. XV:25

FRANZ JOSEF HAYDN
(1681-1767)

(1732-1809)

4

Finale.
Rondo all' Ongarese.
Presto.

TRIO
for PIANO, VIOLIN (OR FLUTE) *and* VIOLONCELLO

F-SHARP MAJOR   FIS-DUR

HOB. XV:26

FRANZ JOSEF HAYDN
(1681-1767)

Finale.
Tempo di Menuetto.

2 3 | 1 2
taptap | taptap

Tempo di Menuetto.

Coda.

TRIO
for PIANO, VIOLIN (OR FLUTE) *and* VIOLONCELLO
F MAJOR F-DUR
HOB. XV:6

FRANZ JOSEF HAYDN
(1681-1767)

Tempo di Menuetto

2 3 | 1 2
ptap | taptap

Tempo di Menuetto

A

MMO Music Group, Inc.. • 50 Executive Blvd. • Elmsford, NY 10523
Call 1.800.669.7464 in the USA • 914.592.1188 International • Fax: 914.592.3575
www.musicminusone.com • email: info@musicminusone.com

MMO 3076

Pub. No. 0981

PRINTED IN USA